Southern
Messenger
Poets

DAVE SMITH, EDITOR

WALT WHITMAN
IN
HELL

WALT WHITMAN
IN
HELL

Poems by T. R. Hummer

LOUISIANA STATE UNIVERSITY PRESS
Baton Rouge and London
1996

Designer: Laura R. Gleason
Typeface: Bembo
Typesetter: Impressions
Printer and binder: Thomson-Shore, Inc.

Library of Congress Cataloging-in-Publication Data
Hummer, T. R.
    Walt Whitman in hell : poems / by T.R. Hummer.
       p.   cm. — (Southern messenger poets)
    ISBN 0-8071-2060-X (cl : alk. paper). — ISBN 0-8071-2061-8 (p)
    I. Title. II. Series.
    PS3558.U445W34   1996
    811'.54—dc20   96-2083
                                                                           CIP

The following poems first appeared in various publications, and are reprinted here with thanks:

Agni Review: "Two Angels Torturing a Soul" (Summer, 1992); *Georgia Review:* "First Assembly of God" (Winter, 1990), "St. Augustine" (Spring, 1996); *Kenyon Review:* "Confusion in the Drought Years" (Spring, 1991), "Greek" (Spring, 1991), "Philadelphia Sentimental" (Spring, 1991), "Walt Whitman in Hell" (Summer, 1993); *Paris Review:* "Friendly Fire" (Winter, 1993), "My Funny Valentine in Spanish" (Winter, 1993), "Scrutiny" (Winter, 1993); *Parnassus:* "Made-for-TV Movie . . ." (Winter, 1993); *Ploughshares:* "Worldly Beauty" (Spring, 1991); *Quarterly West:* "Mechanics" (Spring, 1994) "Ohio Abstract: Hart Crane" (Spring, 1994), "Under the Sign of the Color of Smoke or Stars" (Spring, 1994); *Sewanee Theological Review:* "Apocatastasis Foretold in the Shape of a Canvas of Smoke" (Winter, 1993); *Southern Review:* "The Antichrist in Arkansas" (Fall, 1992), "The Heavenly Doctor" (Fall, 1992), "Plate Glass" (Spring, 1991); *Western Humanities Review,* "December 1909" (Summer, 1993).

    "Ohio Abstract: Hart Crane" was reprinted in *What Will Suffice: Contemporary American Poets on the Art of Poetry,* ed. Christopher Buckley and Christopher Merrill (Gibbs-Smith, 1995).

    "Apocatastasis Foretold in the Shape of a Canvas of Smoke" was reprinted in *The Best American Poetry, 1995,* ed. Richard Howard and David Lehman (Scribner, 1995).

    "Worldly Beauty" was reprinted in *Pushcart Prize Anthology, 1992* (Dustbooks, 1992).

I gratefully acknowledge the John Simon Guggenheim Foundation for a fellowship in poetry that greatly facilitated the completion of this book. Also, for critique, moral support, inspiration, and comradeship, thanks to the following benefactors: David Baker, Tracy Daugherty, Corrinne Hales, Garrett Hongo, Edward Kleinschmidt, Chang-rae Lee, Philip Levine, and Dave Smith.

For Theo

Smokestack lightning
Shining like gold
Don't you hear me calling?

—Chester Arthur Burnett ("Howlin' Wolf")

Contents

WALT WHITMAN
IN
HELL

Zeitgeist Lightning

What were the doctors doing with old Whitman's brain
When it slipped through their fingers? *Anthropometry,*
The biographies tell us: *the measure of* quote
Man unquote—
        weighing and assessing that most god-
Like tumor of consciousness; mapping out the seat
Of the archangel whose occult name is Genius.
A laboratory worker accidentally
Dropped it on the floor.
        Had he put it in a jar?
He was an intern from Des Moines, say, whose mother
Had pawned, well, anything you care to imagine.
Where was his mind? He sat up late the night before
Rereading *Song of Myself.*
        He knew what he was
Up against. And then the lapse, the hideous mess
On the clinical tile. Will he ever forget
The pure mortification of it? Years pass. Conrad
Writes *Lord Jim,* America elects
        Coolidge, Hoover,
Karloff makes *Frankenstein,* in which the doctor's mad
Assistant drops the normal brain and substitutes
A murderer's—and still that humiliation
Goes through him every time
        he closes his eyes. *Fool,*
The body's own voices accuse: *incompetent.*
He was exhausted, worried, overworked, in debt,
Depressed. All beside the point. His shame defines him.
In the Iowa sky
        lightning leaps its mystic
Synapse. Somewhere a war is starting. Nurses stand
At the bedside holding hypodermics, glucose.
Idiot, destroyer! So this is death at last,
Not at all what he expected—
        more disgusting,
More demeaning. Trucks swarm the highway west of town.
Everything is flattened. Now the doctor tightens
The immaculate bolt in his neck, as the brain—
Whose?—throbs in its bloody rhythm.

Yet he can love
Himself completely, even stitched together as
He is. And the rest of us? Where has consciousness
Struck? No matter how we long to drop it, we will
Not crack the convoluted
                    matter of its lines.

Mechanics

Now I begin again to refuse to say the things
    I have refused to say all along:
How trucks on the turnpike raise a seizure
    of passage, a spasm in the plywood walls
Of this room where we lie in refugee heaps,
    too many for the pair of ruptured beds;
How venetian blinds slant radiance down on us
    like sea-illumination falling on certain fish
That mate only in this precise incidence of light.
    One of us is a father: a crowbar
Of neon touches his sleeping face;
    his peace is the stillness
Of the crushed after the bonemill lifts
    its powdery wheel. One of us is a mother:
She lies on her side between him and the wall,
    awake, expecting the shift
Of the sprocket. Many of us are scattered
    bodies of children, some ratcheted
On the second bed, some on the floor:
    dreamers less made of flesh
Than of one anothers' names, driven to this
    bedroom stained with the rainbow
Of factory oil and the darkness that beats
    at the world from inside the lower
Chambers of the heart of Christ. Hours
    from check-out time, the sleeping man
Makes an anonymous sound, a perfect glottal
    echo of 1957, martinis, Edsels on the freeway,
Eisenhower's golf swing, yellow Formica, the residue
    of Korean mortars showering down in the cheap-
Motelroom-cover of night. One child on the floor
    wakes up. His mother took him sleeping
From the backseat of the whipped-out Chevy,
    undressed him, laid him down. Now
He finds himself wearing only his faded
    underwear, and he shivers and whines
For the first time with his own peculiar shame
    at the thought of his naked skin. The mother
Stares at the window as if she could see

a world beyond the chemical light that leaks
Through the blind-slats. She slips out of bed
    and covers her crying son with a sweater.
Something moves in the mirror's half-darkness.
    The shape she sees there could be anyone's,
Living or dead. She thinks she does not care
    what the dead are doing. She knows the dead
Do nothing, exactly like the rest of us.
    They are all on their way somewhere else.
None of them have jobs. This is the only transfiguration
    any of us here can understand: Three days and nights
And the money will be gone. By morning already
    light will come down harder, scarring us
With unconscious brilliance, burning. But now
    the woman feels a tingling in her hands
Where she touched the shrapnel-
    gashed flesh of his belly years ago in the silence
Of a bedroom like this one, and started turning out
    poverty after poverty, each granting itself
The luxury of an *I:* Every stroke of the piston bearing
    body after laboring body in
To the emptiness we call a living.

Compound Light

No one ever shoulders the whole weight of the unconcealed.
Consider my father on the edge of the Western world.
It is 1947. He has won the war. He danced
To Tommy Dorsey, then drove from coast to coast

In a black Ford pickup, trying to clarify his story.
Shadow in starlight. False dawn liquifying on chrome.
The immaculate chain-link fence of the parking lot
Throws down its surgery, its black tracery of scars.

And here is radiance again, coal-stacks hoisting
Their haze above cliffs where cormorants revolve,
Calamari boats diffused in a luminous vapor over the bay.
East of the thumbscrewed mountains, God is torturing

California into consciousness. The tide recoils
From a strand scattered with wheels, pillories, racks,
Skeletons stretched on gibbets. He has been here for hours,
Washed from an anaesthetic motel dream by what he thought

Was the predawn drone of a dynamo, but turned
Into a Coast Guard cruiser winding and rewinding
Its searchlight over the highway, over the town. A silent old woman
Drinks coffee beside him on the spit. They are strangers

In the Pacific spindrift, tourists of insomnia, blind
To what the ensigns will not stop interrogating in the sky.
Morro Rock in this smudge-light looks like Mont-Saint-Victoire
In an unfinished Cézanne watercolor, planes

And patches only, blue and green and white fronting
A pure gray wash, drudging abrasion of surf against seawall.
But the cruiser keeps turning, keeps sending its sodium ray,
And the current falls away. Red lights shift on the flues

Of the hydroelectric plant. Is it cause and effect?
The Pacific goes on disappearing with its residues of mercury.
V-2s ignite in the impure distances of memory.
What can a refugee do with his brass and his khaki?

Time passes. It is sunrise. It could all have been simpler.
The woman with the coffee stares west. She is dressed

Like a fisherman, sleeves rolled up on her forearms.
Just above her wrist, my father thinks he sees a certain familiar

Darkness like a birthmark, a bruise, a tattooed number,
But nothing remains when she shifts subtly toward the light.
She is a tiny woman, ancient, hardly even there.
She is watching the place where the line of the morning sky

Will someday rip itself out of the ocean once and for all—
As if forgetting were the most transparent thing in the world,
As if to live meant anything more than to stumble in the radiance.
Maybe she hears again that voice on the radio drone the chorus

Of the dead between Viceroy commercials and torch songs.
Consider her there with her back to the light, her storyless face
In the shadow of her own will's making. Maybe she thinks
Who is this silent man? If he does not discover

Her name is The Obscure, she will live forever.
Watch the two of them now, how anonymous they are
As the sun detonates through the fogbank and the cruiser stutters.
Someone whistles a love song. It is "Sentimental Journey."

No one now alive remembers the key, or what came after.

Neighborhood Watch: Habeas Corpus

It begins with the pretense of consolation,
    the hallucination of a room—
Calcium dust in the mortises,
    cluster-flies in the walls—

Where years-anonymous lovers
    once strained the thresholds
Of the body. This could be
    one more illuminated

Parchment leaf from *The Book of Images*
    or a high-gloss black-and-white
Photograph fossilized in Lucite:
    Near midnight on Washington St.,

Under the first of the hundred and twenty
    artless moons of the 1980s,
A Shell Oil truck drags its tail
    of a stainless steel chain

Fifty miles an hour along the pavement.
    Through a third-floor
Turret window, I watch it shatter
    the neighborhood. Next door

They drink good brandy and listen
    to "Mack the Knife."
The legal bars shut down
    and the blues begins to happen.

Lawns line this scene with soft
    darkness punctuated by frost,
And the jangling chain
    throws up an aurora of sparks.

From this house beloved
    of carpenter-saints who joined
The flooring boards immaculate
    as cells in honeycomb,

I broadcast the old austerities,
    their edges planed by the centuries

To a microwave's lacerating thinness,
	the attenuated pain

Of a New England winter
	already so far gone in flagellation
Not even Ignatius Loyola could match
	the mortifications of its freezing.

January midnight still has the dull
	near-invisible radiance of plutonium,
The structure of radio static,
	and the blackjack's power to stun.

I contemplate everybody's dying,
	the uncoupling of beauty and breath,
The brutal metrical genius
	of the chromosomes.

Inside the dark cab I arrange,
	the windshield is scrawled
With a white subtext of amphetamines:
	histories, romances, landscapes.

The driver touches his forearm,
	his indigo tattoo
Of a skull and crossbones wearing
	and Uncle Sam top hat.

The legend: *Semper Fidelis.* He knows
	what that Latin sounds like
Shouted by three hundred
	desperate boys in a Marine Corps

Boot camp compound. Cicero, Caesar,
	how much knowledge
Is wasted here? And the homesick
	black recruit from New Jersey,

How he screams when the Corporal takes
	his foreskin with a bayonet
While six others hold him—you can hear
	somebody whisper *Stop crying, nigger,*

Or we'll cut another inch.
	Always faithful. Another billboard

Flashes *Jesus is coming soon.* Jesus
	loves you. Jesus blesses any

Vermont night where nobody sleeps
	until this truck and its corrosive
Tonnage of high-octane Shell passes
	into the jurisdiction of concealment.

All winter I persist in living, as star-colored frost
	cracks granite in the foothills
And the river holds categorical traces
	Orion leaves fossilized in channel-ice.

I am constant in my recitation
	of the silences. I hear lipstick
Inscribing the snifters, courtesy staining the plates,
	whole cliffs of sleet discharging

In the mountains under cover
	of the narrative of domesticity,
The passion of depression. What
	is missing? The icon of a switchblade?

Memento mori? I want to forget
	this country where the law is still
Pristine, where politics dies and comes back
	from the grave as fate. I construct

The urinous light of a jail cell in Burlington
	the moment before the deputy
Slapped me blind. They thought I was drunk
	when the whole time I was nothing

But crazy from eighty hours awake
	at the wheel, and all the white crosses
I'd popped. Later they said I kept screaming
	Habeas corpus, a phrase

From TV courtrooms. What was trying
	to speak through me?
You have the body, I mumble
	in Latin in the moonlight. No priest

Ever told me the mind could be
	this dangerous. What I love

In these nights is the power
    fact has over lyric, how what is

Suffered is suffered, how ice
    resembles ice. Engineers
Call out their snowplows: strange
    rumblings in the streets.

Through the abstracted sky, Arcturus
    flashes its colorless verdict, and we
Go on in our elected houses, living
    this incandescent life apart.

Beyond our windows' blindness,
    the millwheels of clarity crumble
Neuron after neuron into turbulence.
    I assume this illuminated world,

The pure meditation that descends
    when the truck drifts off
The highway, rams a barricade,
    and a hundred tons of sheet flame

Breaches the bulkhead to hammer down
    on conscience like some angelic
Mother tongue. The porch light
    burns out suddenly—no one

Will read this address. Or did you
    expect me to say I have
Faith in something? Whatever gods there are
    have contempt enough for us already.

We are made of next to nothing,
    we understand even less,
And if you torture us even a little,
    we break apart.

Scrutiny

After the D & C, she stood waiting for a taxi
In the clinic awning's shade. It was afternoon in her
Comfortable little city, early rush hour. She could hear
Traffic beginning to swarm under a bloodless bisected moon.
She was watching everything with singular attention,
Men in their wrinkled suits and skin eclipsed by sweat,
The iridescent black of grackles in the gutter, the bright
Chrome and yellow of a '50s Lincoln at the stoplight,
The ambiguous look on the face of God, the shape of her own hands.
And people looked back at her, she thought, with more
Than casual regard, neither sentimental or curious,
But as if they had something disembodied
In common with her. Suddenly she understood how acts
Of attention corrode the world so the flesh feels scraped away,
Worn thin by the action of light, by the eye.
Suddenly she desired another life, a parallel dimension,
Translucent like our own, but in which the dial of consciousness
Is rotated one counterclockwise click, so every mind possesses
The body immediately to the left. At the corner of Second Avenue
And Royal Street, she paid the driver. He watched her as she vanished
Up the steps of the brownstone, a dominion he will never enter,
An allegory whose other side is blankness.

The Heavenly Eunuchs of Rochester

Those who can receive it, let them receive it
—Matt. 19:12

i.

The old accordionist at Casa Vesuvio
Plays "Volare" a dozen times a night
For all the lovers who ask to be remembered.

He's shell-shock hard of hearing—you can feel
The bass from his "Poor People of Paris"
A block away. In the war, he wrote

Ordinary letters from the front while panzers rolled
Over concertina wire out of the cafés
Of Alsace-Lorraine. He plays loud,

And everyone grieves amiably. Through clouded
Plate glass I watch them eat a little ziti,
A little putanesca, the toothless

Dantes of Gibb St. Somebody forks
An artichoke heart and waves it
Uselessly, talking. The heroes are all

Exploded now. Beyond the emptiness
Of history books, they eat veal in heavy
Cream sauce while the glass globes

Of chandeliers fill with a rattle direct
From the dynamos of Rochester
Power and Light. Cloud-banked moon

ii.

In a fixed sky over neutered hills,
The Genesee River ruinous with its ruptured
Cargo of ice—outside the Cadillac Hotel, I try

To make my obsession float
Like an insignificant mist off Ontario.
Nothing but strangers now. Down the block

The tenement where Emma Goldman lived
In 1885, worshiping the "terrible
Nihilist" who shot the Tsar, rots

Into mannered sepia photos—
Her broken-down mule carts,
Canal barges, Masons, the anarchists of Niagara—

Like everything that tries to live here
In the penumbra of the Kodak tower.
Cellists sip espresso in the café

Of the Eastman School of Music,
Gossiping quietly about those self-made mystics
Of the 1960s who'd shatter consciousness

With sweet hits of acid, then stare
Into the burning passage
Of the sun from Capricorn toward Aquarius

Until their retinas vaporized. That was one
Idea of heaven. And now Rochester darkens
With the overthrow of the sublime.

iii.

There is such confusion in the city
While stars prepare their greasefire
Antithesis in the east: More sirens,

More blankness and needle tracks, more
Diesel fumes lifting in burnished blindness
Under the overpass, as I drift

Into the melodrama of light. *Pieces of shit!*
Someone yells through a warehouse door,
And loose coils of rusted cable

Slam the sidewalk, subjectless, intense,
One quantum in the ancient turbulence
Of conscience. Arc-welder acetylene,

Cobalt as an old tattoo, flares out of coal dust
Behind the motor pool. Another afterlife
Becomes a ghetto of spiritual husks, ectoplasmic

Mannequins, memoryless, still outraged
At not being who they say they are.
I am witness only to how sky thickens

Toward this pure sapphire, the critical shade
Of physics, how an old drunk trembles
On the verge of brilliance where the streetlight

Stutters, how the sign in the air incising
CADILLAC HOTEL with its steely
Fluorescent scalpel colors the sidewalk

Clean, the astringent inside a vein,
And nobody feels how much
Is cut away. The scars barely show.

iv.

Cold in this bodilessness, I gather my dream
Of transparency around me, the abstraction
Of warmth that brings itself out of concealment

Under the awning of the Cabaret at the Sign
Of the Man in Armor. Beyond draft-taps
And animated neon clocks, a television screen

Opens its ecstatic little window
Into the other world: flamingos, speedboats,
Football, a universe of angelic boredom.

It gives us its clarity. Through the walls
Of the ruinous lobby of the Cadillac, I see
Carpets go blue as a soul dismantled. In room 600

I left my little human residue—
Old shirts that have taken the heavy shape
Of a body, underwear, a pile of socks,

A used-bookstore novel on the bedside table,
In which one phrase, weathered and finger-smudged,
Is underlined—*Constantinople,*

Where faithless spouses were put in a sack
With hydrophobic cats, and the sack thrown
Into the Bosphorus—a fragment lopped off from the body

Of its discourse. The book is closed,
But these two women touching foreheads
At the window table are not concerned

About its absence; these two young men who lean
At the bar with their hands in each others'
Back pockets don't give a second thought

To what might never be in consciousness again.
They have transgressions and punishments
Of their own to mediate. They watch what's left

v.

Of the sky let down a sentimental snow.
Now whatever remains of consciousness takes
A left turn, into an unlit alley, floating

Toward formal exhaustion, to cultivate
Its own legitimate strangeness behind
The Greyhound terminal. *Terminal,*

Terminal, terminal, drones the woman
By the dumpster. In her schizophrenic chant,
History has no divisions. It could be

1827, William Blake could be dying
Of dyspepsia or consumption or the irony
Of a gnostically fractured heart

In some upstairs bedroom where the humbled
Pane surrenders its clarity to spiderweb
And precipitates of marl. While she waits,

She rummages through empty wine bottles,
Newspapers, boxes, and orange juice tins,
Looking for outtakes from scripture,

Or half of a new pair of boots. *Holy, holy, holy*
Growl the hackneys and the ferries.
Praise to the highest. The gibbet's rigging creaks

The word made light, every second burning
Terrible gaps in the visible.
There are parts of the body so fragile

vi.

They can't survive the simplest acts.
There are people who so hate the body
They don't give a good goddamn.

They gaze into fiery furnaces. They give up
Their eyes to be sanctified. Think of them
Staring straight at the feverish æther.

It must take the courage of the stupid,
The joy of the mystically insane.
From down the street, the twenty-seventh chorus

vii.

Of "O Sole Mio" comes predictably
Full circle as I touch the door
Of the Cadillac Hotel and rattle my key.

The words come so clear, the whole
Restaurant must be singing. Their loss
Is perfectly impersonal. They praise themselves

For their absences and are happy. Through
The cloudy breach their voices open,
An Amtrak engine downgrades toward effacement

In cinematic fog beyond the psychic gates
Of Syracuse, Utica, Schenectady, hauling
Luggage the cracked black leather of another age

Of the world—and down the street, the mounted
Policewoman of Euclid Avenue materializes, waiting
Under the streetlight, under orders, touching

Her nightstick, her androgynous sorrel
A steaming intaglio ground from the neoclassic black
Marble face of the National Savings and Loan.

Blue Alexandrine

At the Church of the Protection of the Holy
Mother of God, three men are hosing down the stone—
One scours the cobbles with a push broom, the others
Slosh caustic on the facade. It steams. There will be
Two funerals later, afterward a slow wedding,
And at midnight the dark young priest will come alone
For a moonlit rehearsal of the litany
Of his sins. But now the air stings with the blue-white
Incense of Lysol. Orthodox, these workmen know
The dignity of their vocation. It is not
God so much as some principal of ablution,
Most pure in April sun, morning, when lilacs stain
The gutters with their wind-bruised blueness: absolute
As a line of light that falls through the sapphire pane
Forming Mary's left eye behind the nave, and spots
A janitor's hand as he dusts the altar—law
Of slaves, ascetics, vultures, surgeons, thieves who spit-
Shine fingerprints from oily brass doorknobs: anti-
Christ of residues: slag-dust, the infinite shit
Of pigeons, grease, all minor holinesses dragged
Through the streets by dogs in every blesséd human
City—Hektor, how they howled for his liver: gone.

Ohio Abstract: Hart Crane

Factory æther thickens over the milky lake at sunrise,
Imperially, like smoke from the last cigar of the Czar.
Bruised faces of stevedores clarify along the docks
As if a metaphysical fluoroscope were touching them

With infiltrating radiation—on the other side, the skeletal
Shape of a crane appears against white buildings.
The tannery whistle agitates. This is inescapably Cleveland.
It is morning now, and the bridge remains the bridge.

Down by the stockyard fence, a man in a pea coat staggers.
He was up all night drinking dago red. A sailor let him
Suck his dick, then blackmailed him for ten dollars.
Now he'll work sixteen hours in a warehouse shifting

Crates of chocolate hearts stamped out for the glorious balls
Of a second-rate midwestern Gilded Age. It isn't the money
That worries him, the thirty cents an hour. It isn't top hats
Or new puce gloves. He can't forget the synaesthesia,

The luminous foretaste of sweat, those syncopated mystical chimes
In the background of his fumbling at the fly-buttons,
The disciplined, improvised slant rhyme of *denim* and *tongue*.
Blinding, the incense of horseshit in the gutter.

He chokes on the ecstatic rumble of the fourth dimension's junk-carts.
Lonely and stupid and sad, the *Don't you love me?* of the barges.
And what are those great water-birds writing down there by the garbage?
In this illusion of space, nothing could ever have existed.

Wrong sex. Wrong sense. Wrong city. Wrong bridge. Wrong life.
But who needs another elegy?. No one ever dies here either.
It just goes on and on, gold foil on an assembly line, two tons
Of hearts for New York City. *Metaphor,* riffs the streetcar,

Is *bear over* in the literal Greek. But who says *what*
Or *how heavy?* Blackjack. Crowbar. Hammer. A man
Coldcocked by the shadow of a telephone pole. Think of all they tell you
The soul holds up in the men's room of the Tower of Light.

Maybe nothing ever meant more on earth than what it weighs.

Somebody's Childhood

They are raising a pillar of smoke
     into the membrane of a winter
Sunset, they are scalpeling the air,
     they are bringing down the legendary oak.

The men build hecatombs
     of brush and branches against
The tissue of the sky. They are lifting
     torches now: their signature

Is a burning that erases the horizon.
     Smoke ascends, a diesel
Sharpness too familiar to recognize.
     It is time to unlearn

The text of the chainsaw, a world
     remade—uglier, more human.
Carry the child to the window.
     It is time for her to fail

To speak first words, the most
     ordinary evils, things better
Than the truth: This enormous man
     eclipsed on the back

Of the tractor, face a murderous smudge
     in the genes: is he a father?
Not to the dead. More likely
     to the never living, strangers

Who might have known, as we
     do not, how to occupy this space,
Take on this flesh. And the others,
     bodies with torches

Twisted shadowless in gasoline-
     infected light?
Even a child knows better
     than to catalog those names.

Gypsum

There is no brilliance in this stone, no artery of light,
No power in its density to illuminate small cities.
I hold the magnifying glass, which is a pure distillation
Of my vision, and stare at the monoclinic crystals,
Less beautiful than quartz, but stranger.
Who would have believed a mineral could sweat?
This is not the weight of diamond in my hand.
I have imagined diamond.

                    It would be massive
Against the palm, significant as a heart,
But with facets honed by eons to a molecule's
Wounding disembodiment. I am nine, not yet flayed
By any brightness, but I have memorized
The hierarchies, longer than the genealogy of God:
Diamond first, then emerald, then ruby, then sapphire—
These are the ones that signify—and after, a whole
Fifth estate of the exotic

                semi-precious. The halls
Of the Science Museum resonate with a colorless dust
Out of Mesopotamia, or desiccated mud from the bed
Of the Ganges. This is *Hands-On Geology for Boys,*
A project of the 1950s. Someday, the museum wall tells us,
All men will be brothers—as soon as cars
Sprout anti-gravity wings and algae splits the atom.
Meanwhile, on another floor, there is *Hands-Off Biology
For Girls, Astronomy*

             for Future Millionaires,
Imaginary Math for Strangers. But here in my palm
Is a gypsum blossom the subtle color of phlegm.
It confounds the lucid categories. *Hydrous calcium sulfate,*
The literature teaches: *Achromatic when pure. Occurs
Massive, or in the form of crystals.* The legend:
$CaSO_4 \cdot 2H_2O$. I consider the faults
And fractures, the splintered crystals, the rose-
Configured false facts

              of matter's story, unclassified,
Imperially singular, the criminal flower of chemistry.
Maybe this is how one mind breaks into another—the way
The teenaged boy from Miami I once read of dreamed

His mother's death, which was happening precisely
At that moment, five hundred miles abstracted,
Or one identical twin went comatose with shock
From the surgery of the other. I already know
Amethyst, peridot, lapis lazuli.
                                        I know chalcedony.
I am learning tiger's eye. Each is hard in my mind.
Each has a cool, specific weight and definite edges.
Soulful. Like the first day I found the hunting knife
In my father's drawer, pulled it from its sheath,
Laid the point against my heart, and knew I held
My peculiar life in my hands—no depressive
Suicidal knowledge, but true and trite
Epiphany, the heart's blood
                                        in the mind's eye
Transcending boundaries of every rank
And phylum. This is how we order things: by a strict
Holy mental violence that tells us the body
Is calcium, iron oxide, diglyceride: it is held
To the earth by a force we give a name
But do not understand: it is conscious
Because it has a brain attached, which may or may not be
The seat of the spirit:
                                        and it possesses as its largest
Single organ the skin—the accident
Of whose pigmentation is one of the most
Irrationally decisive determining factors
In any personal history. Somewhere in this museum
Is a hidden room called *Telepathy for Saints*
Where every occult pain is laid open, every suspect
Micrometastasis is apparent, nobody's birthstone a secret.
But I am tabula rasa here.
                                        What can I know,
Nine years old, a white boy, holding the stone,
Imagining my own annihilation as childhood's shining
Political *gnosis*—trying, like some panicked
Old astrologer, to assign a gemstone to each
Of the heavenly spheres as an allegory for the suffering
Of peasants in Germany's plague-rotted valleys,
For the syphilitic mumbling of princesses in the innermost
Towers of Venice,
                                        for the sorrow of the schizophrenic

Whose chemical voices whisper *Murder them*
Now, in the merciful name of Jesus, and most
For the silent, insistent fear of our museum guard,
A Guatemalan man whose hospital bills keep adding up
To the mystic number that corresponds to onyx?
There is no angelic lineage here, no more definition
Than the knowledge of a half-Cherokee girl
Raped by two Okies
                              for the pure crime of Being,
Or the great-grandson of a Masai chieftain
Beaten blind with a lead-plugged baseball bat
On a midnight street in Queens, or big Swede-blooded boys
Sweating out twelve-hour days in the shallow
Gypsum mines of western New York State, sifting
Truckloads of substrata into what the museum
Guidebook says *Is mainly used as a soil amendment,*
As a retarder in cement,
                              and in making Plaster of Paris.

Caucasian Male, 42

They find the body in the garden back of the jacarandas,
    a stranger beaten beyond simple recognition
With the bludgeon of a carbon-graphite putter.
    In minutes, the watchfires of the suburbs turn angelic,
Searchlights, flashlights, sapphire cloud chamber flash

Of police cruisers on the avenue where predawn executes
    the dew point. French doors light up all over
This neighborhood, clear as laminated isinglass.
    In the beginning there was starlight in open windows,
Music in darkened bedrooms, a virginal odor of milk.

So much forensic mystery in the hands, the teeth,
    the color of the liver. In the pathologist's office
Interrogation commences, flesh required to account for itself
    cell by alien cell. *The icons of childhood*
Were hoarded and set before me, beehives, wheatheads,

Cattle slaughtered in concrete barns. Centrifuges
    spin in the dark of pathology labs.
Shadows of oak trees blur over the gables.
    I was taught the hymn of machinery: auger, tractor,
Cultipacker, harrow, wrench. I was taught to pronounce

Seven holy syllables: Eisenhower, atom bomb. The sense of place
    is changing, the local story shocked
Into a moment of radical revision. Men labor.
    Women labor. Everyone tells everything they know.
We discovered ourselves in hospital beds. We chiseled

Our genealogies on mausoleum walls. An intern lays open
    flaps of muscle: heart membrane alone may yield
A name and a tortured narrative. Nothing suspicious
    in the DNA, nothing in the blood. *I was the one*
In the photograph's center, right of the boy

With amputated fingers, behind the dyslexic girl
    who could not learn to draw the shape
Of the African coast. Fingerprints coalesce
    on computer screens. What matters is method,
The craft of information, logical exhaustion.

Televisions lighten with probable faces. *We filled*
    churches, banks, classrooms. We crowded avenues.
I was given the terms of the law: hunger, territory, gun.
    Golf-cart rechargers hum in garages, reflexive
Circuit breakers laboring to disconnect

The possibilities of loss. *We slept in the blue light*
    of transistors. When we loved, we suffered in our own kind.
All night, school buses rot into sentimental images,
    shadow on an x-ray, cancer on the lung.
Bedrooms echo with motive and alibi. In the vacant morgue,

Automatic lights tick off. *Nothing known,*
    someone has written. *No agent, no ID.*
The coroner assumes that tissue is gathered up
    from the ambiguous track of suns. The attendant
Assumes the soul is the tattoo of the Word

On the idiot thigh of the world. *That was the light*
    of Pure Being we saw revealed in the registers
Of our own flesh. That was the toxin of history we hid
    in our children's names. After sunrise, we will vanish
Into cloudy offices where electron microscopes scan

For the brute contingency of origin, characters inscribed
    on the inner lining of the scrotum, lithograph of identity
At the core of the chromosomes—countersign for pain
    dead Greeks read on the petals of the hyacinth: *ai, ai.*
How could we not believe? We seemed so real.

St. Augustine

I was looking for the return of the body's story, a radical sunrise,
Starbursts over the estuary where fishing boats chafed the yachts—
But I only saw the city's brilliant towers, refinery lights wasting
Silver in the predawn essences. None of us had understood.
In the brain, there is a sensitive blister of images we call the lesion of light.
If I close my eyes on a morning in Florida, I can focus the bed
With its abstract tracery of sheets, the fanatical hotel paintings, the lovers
Still *in coitus,* the woman superior, both of them magisterially lonely.
What I remember is memory itself, breath, the tongue on the skin
Of the thigh, a shadow surrounding the furniture, something that is not
Precisely darkness, but an absence more pure, colorless,
The echo of the blind spot. Confession never happens in the dark.
There is always the naked blinding bulb dangled from the black cliché
Of the cord, the fist and its afterglow. I was talking about my life
In the metropolis of assassins, I was tied to the bed with golden ropes,
And the questions never stopped, the tying and untying of knots.
In the parking lot 27 floors below my hotel balcony, in the middle of the
    night,
A man beat a woman senseless and stole her empty purse.
When morning finally blew in, there were primitive herons mixed up in it,
Astonishing birds the stormy color of ocean, with wingspans wide
As a nine-year-old is tall: real birds, but the sort of image I could believe
Rises out of the deepest caves of memory when a blackjack cracks the
    skull.
Who knows what happens after the brain shuts down?
If you're lucky a thumbprint will glow on the plate glass door
In sunlight, the color of ectoplasm. If you aren't, that song you danced to
In the bar last night will turn up on the elevator's tape loop.
Over the water now, in a sky like the side of a mackerel,
A quarter-moon offers one of its half-lives to the bodiless sunrise,
A celestial residue smeared on the city morning. Seven Stars of David
Painted graffiti yellow on the firmament of asphalt liquify
In the criminal atmospherics of sidewalks' corruption and acidic dew.
A cruiser circles the pavement, its blue strobe corrosive and clean.
But what did the saints have left when their eyes dissolved in holy light?
Nobody's left to testify. The evidence washes away.
Take everything, somebody whispers. *I'll give you anything.*

First Assembly of God

What was it, crosstown, where the bluesman blew riff after riff
And rattled his cup on the curbing, moaning, that made you
Snatch off your cap and look up there, mouth open, breath in the steel
Air of Chicago childhood rising like a Sunday School image of prayer?
You were the one I loved then, the way I wanted to love

Girls on the tenement steps, bums on the corners:
With a godlike purity I no longer understand, an oceanic feeling,
Everything taken literally. It was you who saw it first. How can I tell you
I have long forgotten your name when your image is with me always,
     uplift
Of chin, pulse in the neck, strong line of nose in profile, cap crushed

In one hand against your heart, looking up and pointing?
Three storeys over the street where gangster cars and sepia horses merged,
It glared its bitterness, red paint strafed against brownstone,
FIRST ASSEMBLY OF GOD. You see how it all comes back, like music:
     1934.
We walked those freezing Saturdays needing the bodies of men,

Wanting heat, wanting work. That year there was sweat in the factories,
Sweat in the dark of the slaughterhouse and the groins of the fathers.
And there we were, whatever our names, useless and broke on the street.
What were we, ten? In some other life, I tell you how much I want you
To lower your hand and turn to me. But you pointed up,

You stared, you said *So that's what Protestants do,*
And told me the vision it gave you, an angelic assembly line
Where hieratic ranks of the proletariat hoisted their shining tools
As enormous organs and limbs made their way down the belt, God's body
     still
In its elemental forms: primitive elbow joints, ur-vertebrae, eternities

Of nerves and pipelike capillaries wound on miraculous spools, the greasy
Rush of furnaces in the tunnels of the small intestine,
The lobes of the liver and the mirror-image lobes of the brain
And the circuitry that connects them, the host of crated hands
With their isinglass nails, the nipples in Cosmoline, bolts, the oily nuts,

The inevitable genitalia broken down and packed in excelsior and silk,
All bearing for the first assembly. *My god, there's work for a man,*

You said, your face with its wind-chapped skin alight with the living
   blood,
And I thought of the only Jesus I loved, the icon on my Russian uncle's
   wall,
How the holes in his hands wanted grommeting and the port in his side
   wanted seals:

I looked down the street where the first of the marchers lifted
Under the hammer and sickle their *Workers of the World, Unite.*
I wanted to kneel in front of you, I reached for your arm, but you were
   gone
Into the crowd on the sidewalk where the bluesman's "Love in Vain" was
   lost
In the noise of boots on concrete, sirens, horses and drums, O brother,

Son of dust, cog in the wheel, archetype lover, man.

Friendly Fire

Land war will require the most complex
combat flying ever flown, with more
tragedies of friendly fire inevitable.
                    —CNN newscast, 2/4/91

Heraclitean, for instance: the world as a gaseous
Shimmer, like afterburner fumes in the oily night sky
Outside Carbondale, where lovers pass through the flux
Of the heart's napalm—or alchemical: the transformative image
Of the sun over Dallas, antiseptic if you could touch it,
Tritely ætherial, the volatile gold of gas-well burn-off
On the freeway's horizon, cauterizing, uncorrupting bone—
We could imagine anything. Suppose we pulled a lever
And every carburetor in Charlottesville
Detonated in a transcendental rush of vesicatory gas
And oxyacetylene? What would we think we were seeing?
What residue would remain?
                              I think it would be elemental.
I think it would be pure. I think it would give off the smell
Of brass, chrysanthemums, caustic old velour—
Or that strange metallic odor that drags my grandmother's face
Up from the flare of my neurons, where the innocent dead all go:
A bombed-out country no body belongs to, untouchable, chemical, clean.

Philadelphia Sentimental

Conduits and overwrought fire escapes. Icons from Little Italy.
Rifted backstreets of Hungarian strangers in the aura
Of diesel and hops. "Unchained Melody" leaks
From a ghetto blaster some ghost of a teenager shoulders
Round and round the neighborhood, the music grown slowly

Ubiquitous. They have drunk Vouvray from a tumbler,
They have eaten fruit from a bowl—the fig-skins darkening
In candlelight, cantaloupe rinds stained with raspberry
Sweetening degree by degree toward the rich half-life
Of compost. They made love slowly while freight trains

Stalled beyond the alley. There was rain, then moonlight
Bled through the clouds' exhaustion. They slept and woke
And slept again. They lay dreaming, joined at the solar plexus,
Barges dense with pig iron stoking and shifting
Against the Delaware's face. On the bedside table, a gift:

A small wooden earth that opens, and inside nests
A zodiacal orb inside which a Renaissance sun contains
A medieval moon with the face of Our Lady of the Menses.
It is early morning now. Light the color of pale urine
Weakly touches me where I hover looking down at them.

None of us is here for the simple sake of beauty.
The real is what is in the soul and what is outside the soul.
Maybe I am the angel of memory, or maybe they are. Who knows?
I prophesy garbage trucks in the alley, trepidation of the spheres.
There will be old love songs on the airwaves,

Accidents, sirens, and smoke. Some will say an eagle
Flew over the city with a serpent choked in its claws,
And everyone looked up and marveled—some will believe
Lions walked the streets at noon. But these two who sleep
Beneath me, each wrapped in the cliché of someone else's arms—

From here, I can see the past write itself on their skin in scars.

Made-for-TV Movie, in Which a Couple Throws a Copy of Frederic Jameson's *Postmodernism; or, The Logic of Late Capitalism* off a Bridge and into a River

i.

Not out of disrespect, but not in worship either,
Though the gesture could be read each way, depending on your assump-
    tions.
It is just that spring has come again, and the water has the depth of field
Of snowmelt. When traffic subsides, the stone bridge goes on trembling.

ii.

The town is familiar: storefronts, post office, movie house
Where three films are showing, the posters in their cases out of focus.
People pass by. The place has a background hum
Like the magnified sound of a beehive tracked through a synthesizer.
These two on the bridge are dressed identically: blue sweatshirts, faded
    jeans,
And they both feel exotic euphoria as they watch the whole flow
Of the river unspooling beneath them.

iii.

It is like a suicide pact, or a symbolic revolution.
They throw the book off together. It does not flutter in the air—
It drops like an anvil, sinks instantly out of sight.
This appears to be New England, where rivers are small but intense.
Likely the town had a mill once. Twenty yards downstream
There's a ten-foot drop-off, an artificial spillway.

iv.

At the local bistro, they share lunch: *bourbon shrimp*
With linguini the menu says, *7 jumbo shrimp flamed*
With bourbon and tossed with cream, scallions, and spices.
Through tinted restaurant plate glass, they can see the water foaming.
The book lies on the table. In the mountains above the courthouse,
At the heart of the rotting snowpack, the structure of ice
Is giving way, hydrogen bonds collapsing.
Granite contracts. Quartzite crystals splinter.
The roots of herbs break down: angelica, belladonna, death camas.

All morning they stayed in bed, a Sony camcorder
Set up on a tripod by the bureau. They were taping themselves
An alternate *Kama Sutra,* a sort of homemade Bible.

v.

The book is dense, but you'd think it might float, like so much
Fouled in the current: Styrofoam, drowned squirrels, condoms,
The bole of an ancient maple washed down in the April flood.
You'd think there might be a visible difference when it vanishes,
Or some special sound when it slips from the lip of the dam.
One of them has read it, one of them refused. They've been lovers
For a year. They have their own dialectic. In the bedroom, they kissed
Each others' breasts while the camera whirred and clicked.
They've talked it over. They've studied the illustrations: Van Gogh's

vi.

A Pair of Boots, Walker Evans' photograph of work shoes.
They are very different, but very much alike. Pairs,
And pairs of pairs. The problem is, they have no story.
The problem is, one of them is lost. You'd think
There might be some special sorrow. On the bridge, they talk
Of the man they know who lives in a trailer in the mountains,
How he comes home alone now, parks his gas truck in the ruined driveway,
Turns the TV on, drinks beer, and passes out. He watches himself
In dreams each night behind the blue electronic flicker:

vii.

The one about the deer hunt, the one about the Spanish blonde.
To them, his life is predictable and sad. That is one category,
Like the lives of farmers: *pastoral.* And the lives of shopkeepers: *bourgeois.*
One of them was married once. One of them refuses
The edges things drop over, the dark current in which things dissolve.

viii.

Somewhere else, there is gunfire on the soundtrack.
Somewhere else, the strained heart, the muscles of the inner thigh,
The inscribed surface of the forehead, the ruptured uterus
Signify. Is that the old life we dream we are losing, comrades,
The old morality we thought we loved, the pedagogy, the classic
Didactic art? Just change the channels. There is Pound still scattering

Pigeons around the Roman fountains, Le Corbusier
Constructing elitist Utopian space, Virginia Woolf turning
Into a terrible man and back again, and a couple

ix.

Of daffodils lifting themselves over and over out of the bankrupt soil
On the opposite shore, caught in their perpetual visionary dreariness.
The river rumbles familiarly. One of the women frames
A false photograph with her fingers. If she only had her Nikon,
The light meter, the polarizing filter, she could fix

x.

Her lover with this pre-Raphaelite aura of April sunlight in her hair—
And the book, just before it vanishes in the current, might make
A statement if you could see it
In high-contrast black-and-white, in a Plexiglas frame.

Plate Glass

Over this city of transparent buildings, the zodiac staggers, bombed
On mercury and the vapors of naphthalene. One more unimaginable
Down-And-Out Year Of Our Lord has come and gone
When Houston, Texas, tossed its crutch and limped toward heaven
In robes of polyester and rhinestone, still unhealed.
The melancholy that rises now from the entropy of the Cotton Exchange
Is worthy of the brilliant self-indulgence of a Keats.
But that woman on the avenue is the cropduster's lover. She believes
In a universe the size of the palm of a hand, worlds you can snuff
With a single gesture, like the sun. She has flown in a yellow biplane,
Trailing clouds of herbicide, occluding malls, galleries
Of overpriced landscapes, tiny refineries. Her pilot tied down the stick
With binder-twine and scrambled to the forward cockpit
Where she waited with her blouse undone for the password
To the city physic and the city psychic, the *genius loci* of the vision
Of street-sweepers and seraphim, *gnosis* at 6000 feet.
From where she hovered, ghettoes appeared vivid as needlepoint.
The ruined shack where Lightnin' Hopkins was born assumed
The lineaments of a tragic miniature, the detail of fine cloisonné.
Architects who stood on the sixtieth crystal floor of Mobil Oil
Watching her loop and roll into the æther of the profit margin
Suddenly realized transcendence is of point of view. In a flash,
They understood how, for centuries, the thunderheads were changing
From spirit to water, from hurricane to distillate of acid, an image
With multiple forms in the light. But here and now she stops like anyone
On the sidewalk in front of a Neiman-Marcus window
Under the blinding Texas sun, staring in at priceless platinum
Corkscrews, the metal still burning from the crucible and the anvil,
At laser-powered toasters, holographic lingerie, his-and-her
Sports cars with windshields deadened the gray of lead alkali.
Beside them, she recognizes a perfect scale model of Houston
Crafted of resonate crystal calcite and carved dry ice
Whose CO_2 vapors rise heavenward in polarized mimesis
Of fluorocarbon haze, shimmer of argon and Treflan.
She tries to make out a tiny image of herself on the sidewalk
In front of plate glass, staring in, trying to discover an even smaller self
Staring farther in—but there is only absence where she thinks she is,
Regression, inviolate light. She believes it could be simpler than it is
To know the real, if only the names of things were what they ought to be.

But when she turns and looks up, distracted by the old-fashioned sound
Of a biplane's engine stalling out of sight, she thinks she reads the fading
Signature of God etched backward in Art Deco gold leaf
Against the nosemarked storefront of the planet.
Someone is skywriting there, but she can't make out
What she has every right to believe is hers, something about love
And the world's being made and remade in the shape of her desire—
The content of rhetoric being purity, she being one of the chosen.

—for Edward Hirsch
and after Barthelme

Under the Sign of the Color of Smoke or Stars

On the edge of this California city, there is a smell in the air
Like the sulphurous burning of midnight artillery flares.
Things are arranged here, I think, according to the will of the light,
Perfected by refraction, magnified, obscured. Rooftops,
Chemical silver, give off slaty radiance. Beyond the ridge, the bark
Of a eucalyptus shimmers, reflecting a texture like the newsprint skin
Of an ancient Vietnamese woman's body once it is shuttered
Through the diamond-blue closeup lens of a Leica, blown up
In the darkroom, printed in high contrast.
                                        At the restaurant
I ate lavishly, with chopsticks. *In the Year of the Rat,*
The fortune cookie said, *Everything is simple. In the Year of the Snake,*
Who knows? And after, because I thought there was no one,
I walked above the suburbs, heavy with rice and duck
And melodramatic doubt.
                        Lovers stumble on this hillside
Under the smoggy belt of Orion. Below us, the valley floor constellates,
A computer-animation portrait of the surface of the cortex, idiot flesh
Transfigured by the ganglion–flash of sodium light, neon, and traffic.
The sky breaks open with incendiary brilliance.
There is napalm and the sweetness of morphine.
This is the poisonous future of the Scorpion,
The memory of the Crab—sideways, clawed and nerveless.
Everywhere I look, the center of consciousness
Is flaring through the ozone breath of the mountain,
Miles westward, into the sparked darkness we call
The Pacific.
            It's too late now to start for the other world—
Only barely, but nevertheless. This body would vortex
A millisecond before I crossed the line, and its emptiness would suck me
Through whatever milky purity blossoms between here and the constella-
    tions,
Back into the fatal whiteness of the flesh I started from.

My Funny Valentine in Spanish

In the 7-11 parking lot, white boys are terrorized
By a Lincoln stereo punching out 98-decibel jazz. The scene
Reminds them unconsciously of high-art cinema shot
In ferocious blue illumination: the deep wax-job
Of the Continental telegraphing the luster of the streetlights,
The stone-colored lawyer in an elegant linen jacket
Leaning on the fender while the digital self-service pump
Carries on its decisive artifice. Turned up this loud
Past midnight, Miles Davis is a cool apocalypse
Like nothing these boys on stolen skateboards ever entered,
A neighborhood in which no one remembers the depth
Of the æther where antifreeze and motor oil pool,
Or the white ghosts of congressmen obliterating angels' hairs
With their otherworldly logic. This is the music they play
In the tunnels of the underground where subways run
From Cambodia to East L.A. In the barrios, children speak
The subjunctive—*If this were bread, could one eat it?*—
And the love of God is a drug, like the love of death.
The *abuela* behind the 7-11 counter shuffles
And lays out the cards. Her *abuela* taught her this.
Five of clubs, three of diamonds: Every low card
Whispers its password and its alibi. There's an occult
Future here. Somebody makes it. Somebody loves somebody
And crosses the great water for a promise, on a dare.
Rodgers & Hart. The boys on their skateboards listen
To the trumpet whose language nobody taught them.
Mi enamorada graciosa, it might be singing. *Mi corazón.*
One morning somebody wants to blast somebody's lights
Into a pure cobalt vapor floating at the Pleiades' heart,
One morning the cash register and the Lotto machine are eclipsed
By a mist of tear gas–shadowed perfume, the exhaust of the LAPD.
And one morning—Neruda made it past tense in invincible Spanish
That could not translate Franco into hell, or contradict
The bullets that distorted Lorca—*Everything is aflame,*
One morning the fires/Come out of the earth/Devouring people.

—*for Philip Levine*

The Antichrist in Arkansas

At the edge of town, day lilies the gold of old whiskey
Move tonelessly. At the margin of the courthouse shadow,
A little sky gives off its one unchanging line.
It is written in the Gnostic *Gospel of Truth* that life is nightmare,
As if people were murdering them, though there is no one
Even pursuing them, or they themselves are killing
Their neighbors, for they have been stained with their blood.
Let there be a little clarity here, let the light arrive,
The way the dynamite train rolls into Arkadelphia:
An overwhelming ablution, a scheduled breakdown.
In the crib behind the cotton gin, three of them are gathered.
In the alley off Jefferson Street, they are giving secret signs.
Who are they? Call them the Brotherhood of Darkness.
Give them emblems: khaki workshirts, Prince Albert in a can.
They live in clapboard temples set up in the taboo precincts,
They worship at the Synagogues of the Flesh of the Holy Pig.
Mornings, hours before sunrise, they kneel at the open flame;
Past midnight, if you wake in an impure sweat, you can hear
Their pentatonic psalms sift through the veils of the juke joints.
You who are uninitiate, you who walk the sunlit bricks
Of the Main Street sidewalk past the bank to the hotel café,
You of the regimental necktie, you who render
Unto Woodrow Wilson, live in the obvious houses,
Drive Fords, dance to "Arkansas Traveler"—Brotherhood of Light,
You think the fields at least are innocent, gathered without
The rhetoric of pastoral, the flat farmland, the plows
Moving in the middle distance; you believe at least
In the trees, gone in their green brooding. But in 1919,
83 bodies were given to druid oaks on the fringes
Of these blesséd little cities: Conway, Fort Smith, Fayetteville,
West Memphis, El Dorado, Pine Bluff, Forest City,
The mecca of Hot Springs. How many know
The ritual formula that exorcises unclean flesh?
How many have learned the arcana, the knotting
And unknotting of hemp? So it has been written
In *The Paraphrase of Shem,* and quoted
In *The Little Rock Gazette: Nature turned her dark vagina*
And cast from her the power of fire, which was in her
From the beginning, through the practice of darkness.

Look: already the evening brightens, already the locomotive
Crosses the valley in a shimmer of pure entropic heat.
Everything in the flesh converges. In a moment it will be too late.
Gather them up, believer. Put them on the backs of mules.
Take them where the wind completes its broken sentence
Of damnation against the elder, against the ash.
The secret is simplicity: pray to me, the spirit who steals
The breath of the one whose feet no longer touch
The ground; make sacrifice to the god who silences him
Whose testicles bleed in his own unsanctified mouth.

Confusion in the Drought Years

All along, there was thirst shaping up in the uterine rot of fence posts
Everywhere the sunlight touched. All along, the fieldhands' sweat
Was ominous with salt. *Sister,* the preacher told me,
I believe there is brilliance coming.
Sister, he said, *we will lay all our burdens down.*

But across the fields I could see the heatwaves' aura
Over the hood of the laboring tractor, covering my brothers' faces like a
    caul,
And the pastureland revealed itself with its clumps of holy scrub oak
Where the cattle gathered in what shade there was, worshipful and dumb.
I closed the book in the preacher's face, I took his hands away

From the buttons of my dress. Through the window, I watched
The bodies of cornstalks martyr themselves in dustdevil pyres of topsoil.
Sister, the preacher whispered, *Sister,* but I left him naked
In the bruise-colored shade of the parlor. What of all the saints
Who burned their beautiful hair in the rapture of the *auto-de-fè?*

I went into the dooryard where the columbines were wasting their blooms.
I could hear the haybalers beyond the horizon wind and unwind their
    hymn.
Some claim visions, the prayer books say, but I see what I see,
I believe what all believers remember: the past and the time to come.
Preacher, a clay road spools this prairie where invisible combines lift

Astral bodies of wheatdust against the sulfate glaze of the morning sky.
Hardwoods sawtooth the horizon: oaks, old worthless elms, all ash
Now, all consumed in the mind, like carcasses of crows
The brothers shot in the orchard—what else to do but burn them?—or
    down
The old woman plucked in the barnyard, bloodying dead breasts

For featherbeds. Who was she? Somebody's grandmother?
And the lovers she has forgotten, what fumes trace their vapor trails?
Preacher, this world we have come to—it wants to go on without us,
All solstice, pure angle of sunlight. But the father who appears in the
    grove,
Tall among beehives, pumping the smoker's bellows, releases a cloud

Of numbness into heartwood, and the son on the tractor turns the color
Of oil on steel, and the sister in the dooryard remembers how years from
    now
She will stitch the ticking by candlelight, kneading feathers
Into the body-shape of our oldest desire: To leave a mark on everything
    clean
We can find, perversity, the deep-etched signature.

The Heavenly Doctor

Against phthisis. Against hysteria, scoliosis, quinsy.
Acute to the rhythm of the womb's trepidations, morphology of rupture,
Circumcision, leeching, the inhaling of chloroform during labor.
Indentured to disease and infirmity. Dedicated to radical cure.

Against chronic bronchitis and laryngitis: opium smoke.
Against neuralgic affections and rheumatism: the same and again the same.
About death, nobody knows anything, no matter what they tell you.
In Milan, they say a corpse can be consumed in twenty minutes

By a stream of hot air at white heat, for about $3 cost—nothing left
But a little heap of snow-white ashes: As when the meteor passed
In the early morning, and, fading, threw
A sudden glaring into my room like a flash from a hunter's firepan.

Against delirium, the mirrors and smoke of the will.
Case of parturition, ordinary, $50 or more.
Administering an enema, $5. Bleeding, $1. Cupping, $2 or more.
Administration of chloroform during surgical operations, $5 or more.

In this world, saws and the fever—in the next, gauze and morphine.
Against gangrene: amputation. As on the day
The Wadesborough Bridge was cut down and the Spencer Tucker Bridge
Was burnt by order of Colonel Miller, the military commandant,

Whom may the Devil confound for the act.
There on the embankment we found a dozen or more
With inconceivable wounds. I sawed off five arms and six legs
While dragonflies phosphoresced in the breeze on the river

And twelve white herons made the astrologer's wheel in the air overhead.
Against beauty. Against all that beauty portends.
Against any fool who believes in free will or an afterlife.
Against Mysticism, Hedonism, Stoicism, Episcopalianism.

Against heaps of undifferentiated flesh rotting in the sunlight.
In *The London Scalpel,* the world's highest medical authority,
I have read the following, given as an infallible cure
For smallpox and scarlet fever: sulphate zinc, one grain;

Foxglove digitalis, one grain; half a teaspoonful of sugar; mix
With two teaspoonsful of water; take a teaspoonful every hour.

It states that either disease will disappear in half a day.
It states that if countries compelled their doctors to use this,

There would be no need for pesthouses.
Against all such desperate lies, however well-intentioned.
Against nature, corruption of the flesh, the body's subversion.
Against philosophy, which is nothing but the history of our fragmentation.

Against fatherhood, patriots, pride of war, saber and Minié ball.
Against the human race, which could have ended millennia ago,
Or in any age, by radical celibacy, if everyone on the planet
Would but accede to it. Against knowledge, physical or metaphysical,

Which leads to nothing but this: The soul is flesh. Do as little as you can.
Vis cogitativa, the power of sense: Watch cloud formations change.
Vis rememorativa, the power of memory: Don't turn your back on your
    brother.
Brimstone fumes kill every species of fungus in plant, beast, and man.

Case of abortion, actual or threatened only, $25 or more.
Case of syphilis or gonorrhea, $20 or more *in advance.*
For the blind poor, Rx: bleed. For yourself, Rx: love nothing.
Sow rows of onions only. Plant turnips in the dark of the moon.

December 1909

. . . on or about December 1910 human character changed.
—*Virginia Woolf*

Snow on granite, sleet-rind the tincture of nickel,
Sun at the western horizon cataract-pale: the world's
Steely body hisses like gas in a streetlamp
Turning dark, going down.

      The woman obsessed
With a bridge rail, the man who washes his hands,
Meet on the sidewalk, exchanging mannerly bows.
She imagines a coil of rope—one end tied to the trestle,
The other trim around her neck—how it would accelerate
With her mass, unspooling its thirty-two feet per second
Per second squared toward the unreachable black inertia
Of river. She dreams of the paralyzing snap.

         The man, too,
Is in love with water. He stands at the sink
A dozen times an hour, scrubbing immaculate stigmata
Into his soapy palms. On the street he wears
Gloves of close-grained leather. When he peels them back
Like a foreskin in his dark bedroom, the underflesh
Resurrects its openness in sterile bleeding.

          All over the city
It is still the Golden Age, a year with its winter that scatters
Sleet like bone-shrapnel over the rotten shakes
And slate-sloped rooftops of an order already gone
Five million years into sexual wreckage. Everywhere
Consciousness is catastrophic and brilliant with ordinary love.
He looks at her as he would at any stranger,

        wanting a world
So pure no one would need to touch or eat or breathe
Uncleanness, the body winter-bitten to a frost like decorous ash.
Her Gibson-girl hair scintillates, diamonded with ice.
She acknowledges his careful *good day* with an instressed smile.
The future is revealed to her. It is black and supercooled
Like a river on a Christmas midnight, too quick-running to harden.
Maybe the shape of her mind never changes,

        maybe it remains

Monotonous and varied as a crystal lattice. Or maybe it gutters
Like gaslight in a sheer December whiteout—center to circumference,
Nucleus to godhead—toward annihilation, forever the same.

Greek

Hard now to remember those winters, snow scabbing the stones
Outside Gettysburg ten years after the names sank in with the carcasses.
What did I know about the unities? It was freezing, we had nothing,
We'd eaten the mules, the wheatfields were scattered with salt.
I hunched in the seminary balancing the leatherbound Euclid
Against the Homer my father had scribbled his name in once, a boy
Like me, still ignorant and alive. Outside, Pennsylvania was a hellish
Polygon of ice. *The opposite sides and angles of a parallelogram*
Are equal to one another, and the diagonal bisects it; that is, divides it
Into two equal parts. I imagined him repeating these things
Twenty-five years ago in a body smaller than mine.
I imagined him in the ground, the ground bisected, two worlds
Divided, the line drawn between him and me.
Things which are equal to the same thing are equal to one another.
I would take up the ministry that laid him down. I would speak the Word
That choked him. His body after ten years under was less than mine,
A volume of icy grit surrounding a Minié ball. We were learning. I knew
History was doing the same things others had done, being born,
Sweating, fighting, saying axioms by rote. I drew the geometry
Of fields in early spring, dead men at the plows,
Forty acres of ground chiseled and harrowed, laid out naked in the sun.
I know now they died of everything you can think of: Evisceration, shock,
Peritonitis, gangrene, malnutrition, incompetence, deceit,
Every possible loss. Then, I knew only what we copied
From the poet and translated: *The spear in his heart*
Was stuck fast, but the heart was panting still and beating
To shake the butt end of the spear. In the freezing house, my mother
Was sewing trousers, running her ruined fingers over the parallel lines of a
   bolt
Of corduroy, burning her hands on linen, stitching, shivering,
A conventional emblem of loss. *If equals be taken from equals,*
The remainders are equal. How could she weave him back? She had no
   loom.
She made uniforms for soldiers. They taught us to say these things:
My father in the underworld is bloodless, wanting nothing.
What is a nation to him? What is a son? There are rivers, stinking fires,
Ghostly pain like the pressure of starlight, emptiness, illusion,

There are six hundred thousand souls repeating their indifference every
    second
In the Hades of the Brothers' War. He is a citizen of that polis now,
And I hate him in the language of the dead I am still learning slowly
For the sake of his memory, sign by inevitable sign.

Apocatastasis Foretold in the Shape of a Canvas of Smoke

At the left edge of the field of vision, a stooped woman dumps
Steaming water from her galvanized bucket against a granite wall.
In this meditation, she might be an emblem of genocide

Or simply somebody's grandmother dumping dishwater in the snow.
Gray earth, gray sky—the brushstroke of the horizon visible
Only to someone who knows what to look for, pure

Transparent style. The water is a soapy broth of tea dregs,
Grease, and lye, which the wormy dog that hides
Under her skirt licks from the frozen stones. Its every gesture

Is an archetype, something that could be perfectly described only
In Indo-European. In the middle distance, from the indistinct
Shadow of a minor mountain, there is hazy motion, possibly an army:

The sound of leather groaning, silk-muffled hammers
Of the temple builders, adze-chafe, pneumatic saws, the crack
Of a splintering axletree. The dog's ruff is the same shade of silver

As the metal of her bucket, and the water the bucket holds,
And the vapor that rises off the frost-etched stone of the wall.
Her old dress bunches at her belly in an intaglio like stretch marks.

She had children, and those children died. She had children,
And those children had children. Where is the nostalgia
For humanity? Where are all the stories we have learned

To interpret so perfectly? You may think there is tragedy here,
But this is only the beginning. In the gunpowder haze that lifts
Over the boundary-ridge, and in the bucket's mural of steam,

The characters gather: a man who lifts his handful of blood
To the vacuous spirit he knows is his mother, and she drinks
And speaks his name, and is oblivion. Look

Where the machinery of heaven drags form after form
Out of this sarcophagus God carved from the onyx cliff-face of being
And hinged with elaborate craftsmanship into the joinery of her spine,

So when the latch clicks and the lid of her body swings open,
Another rises luminous and whole into the expanse of unconcealment.
It comes almost to nothing. Winter is here, and the half-starved

Cattle still give milk, though it is thin, with a tinge of vein-blue.
February sleet spits on flagstones with the noise a bronze knife makes
Against hickory. The carver at his bench is gouging another bowl

For goats' blood, while the dog in the culvert gnaws
Whatever rat he can find, then curls his carcass in on itself
Like a Möbius strip for warmth, everything drawn together.

Worldly Beauty

Skin deep, you son-of-a-bitch, I thought, *no more*—but the impure
Tip of his needle tracked its dance. The snake between the ribs,
Anchor, tiger, the daggered heart, *memento mori* of the skull:
In the heat of the body's refusal,

                            I had to choose among images.
Beyond the window, awl-points of sun incised
San Francisco Bay with patterns of blindingness. I watched
The sea over his shoulder as he touched me with his tools,
The chisel made of the bone

                        of an albatross, narrow,
Very sharp, driven by means of a little mallet—or
An oblong piece of human bone, *os ilium,* an inch and a half broad
And two inches long, one end cut like a small-toothed comb,
The other, fastened to a piece of cane,

                         like a serrated adze.
He leaned above me, rubbing the pigments in,
His own skin clean and golden, untouched by signs or tokens,
No fire on the lake, scarlet penis in a secret place,
No swastika, *rosa mystica,*

                  no lightning or transparent eye.
He wore no shirt. He was fat as a Buddha. His fleshy nipples
Hung like incipient breasts. How long could I authorize this pain?
I stared at snapshots on the walls: images of the carriers of images,
Those who had come here before me,

                        done this thing and lived.
One was a man, on his chest the cod, split from head to tail,
Laid open; on each thigh the octopus, and below each knee the frog.
One was a woman, on her breast the head with forepaws of the beaver;
On each shoulder the head

                 of the eagle or thunderbird;
On each arm, extending to and covering the back of the hand,
The halibut; on the right leg the bullhead; on the left leg the turtle.
I sat on my small stool, my blouse drawn open. I suffered
The alcohol and the burning, in love

                    with the clean
Lines of boats on distant water, the absolute
Whiteness of sailcloth, anesthetic sting of brine.
I knew I could take the blueprint of the broken tower on my skin,

The profile of the angel of blood.
                                    I knew I could carry another flesh
On my flesh, go otherworldly as any bodily shape, male or female,
Become a terrible breathing heap of descriptions of God.
In that dirty parlor on the western edge of the empire of the chosen,
I finally refused it all—the romance

                              of the past, the heaven of family.
I denied the apocalypse of genes, the passionate resurrection
Of memory, the pierced and reborn body we call *the story*
Of our lives. In his hand, the needle's spasm repeated itself.
He sweated. He held the mirror.

                              What does it matter now
Who I say I am? This may not be done in the presence
Of the dead, or if anyone in the house should dream of floods,
Lest there be excessive bleeding—this may not be done if a man
Should dream of the face of a woman, or a woman

                                    of the face of a man,
Lest the shape of another self should shiver between
The soul that is and the soul that is to come. I am the image
Of diesels on the Embarcadero, I am the image of water—
So much beauty, and the world is still

                              only the world.

Two Angels Torturing a Soul

Deny nothing. Say yes to the whole of the earth.
    Concede us the aura of starlight in alleyways
Where nightsticks come down. The burnished leather belts
    Are heavy with metal: bright steel and blue-black steel,

Handcuffs, badges, whistles, Smith & Wessons.
    Spill everything. Grant it the simple dignity of a name.
On the assembly lines of the surgical arenas
    They are holding nothing back. In the confessional booths

Of the CAT scan, they are revealing all they know.
    Forget your justifications. What is memory to you?
Truths are projected in cobalt. There is laying on of hands.
    You imagine your story as the quick sapphire skin

A blue racer looped and left in Möbius coils under the gate,
    Immaculate in the clarity of this life's illumination?
You ought to have seen the mind is the half-life of punishment,
    Its cancerous image. You ought to have understood fluorescent light

Splintering off the chromium rails of a hospital bed
    Is no alibi for the holy. On the sidewalk in front of a café,
In the museum parking lot, in the ghetto at the end
    Of the medulla oblongata, God sets his net to drag his enemies in,

His rope which means protection. Deliver him three times
    The life in the body, his perverse awareness.
You ought to have known the son-of-a-bitch was after you.
    You are what he dreams when he dreams of heaven.

Walt Whitman in Hell

. . . on the black waters of Lethe?
　　　　—Ginsberg

In the second circle—the level of perpetual dysfunction
Where untouchable lovers are damned by definition
To read each others' stories over and over

In voices like monotonous tape loops repeating forever
The lessons of the *Book of the Unabridged Living Body*—
The interior lights of a downtown express strobe

Grand Central platform and vanish, leaving nothing
But a retinal afterglow of the Lexington Avenue line.
Engines push tarry winds out of the heavy darkness

Of the tunnels. They break like punished hurricanes
Into the station's wintery light. I carry a map
Of this place in memory only—uptown, downtown,

Crosstown—capillaried in the visual mind,
Terminal names a systole and diastole of space
That contracts and relaxes around me when I think of it,

Including everything, the whole corporeal ghost
Of Manhattan and beyond. But where is anything, really?
Do I dare trust memory's directions? Or is this the first

And most damning despair, that it all may be nothing
But dots, biochemical flashes, swampgas waverings
Of imaginary light, the meaning of this landscape

Of ashes simply being that I have to wonder
What it means, and thereby recall myself?
And as if this uncertainty were one of the most sublime

Angels of torture, I am suddenly empowered
To remember the mountains, hills, and gorges
Of Manhattan, where the gates of the subways appear

To the sight like holes and clefts in the rocks,
Some extended and wide, some straitened
And narrow, many of them rugged—they all,

When looked into, appear dark and dusky;
But the spirits in them are in such a luminosity
As arises from burning coals. Someone

Among them plays a saxophone—no, someone scats
A bebop riff in a voice so skewed by sterno
It comes through sounding like brass,

And modulates into the Lydian mode:
Someone of them remembers *A Love Supreme,*
And this is my signal, I go down, and everything begins.

It is given now that I realize what comes first,
The station of instruction, the 81st St. entrance
On the Avenue of the Americas line. I enter

From the basement of the Museum of Natural History,
Where passing over is a simple fact, no astonishment,
Because overhead is a whole granite houseful

Of *memento mori*—tombstones, mummies,
And the icthyosaur's whatmeworry grin. The way here
Is wide and smooth, passing over is a token

I buy from a woman in a Plexiglas cube,
Passing over is a slot and the click of a turnstile. It is here
The man with the methyl voice sings Coltrane and passes out

Pamphlets enumerating the seven words that mean
The body thinking: Thumos, Phrenes, Nöos, and *Psyche,*
All of them translated variously from Homeric Greek

As *mind* or *soul*—and *Kradie, Ker,* and *Etor,*
Rendered often as *heart* or *spirit.* But all
The translations are wrong, I read, entirely:

These must be thought of as objective parts
Of the body, the pamphlet tells me, understood
As my first clue that I am leaving

Anything behind. I embody now the plains and valleys
Of Brooklyn near the foot of the Brooklyn Bridge,
Where the subway gates resemble dens and caverns,

Chasms and whirlpools, bogs, standing water—
And when they are opened, there bursts from them
Something like the fire and smoke that is seen in the air

From burning buildings, or like a flame without smoke,
Or like soot such as comes from an explosive chimney,
Or like a mist and thick cloud: it is here the woman

With a face like a drowned suicide's crouches
At the first turning of the downward stairway
I can't help choosing, holding up her autocratic

Homemade sign: I AM A VICTIM
OF THE CONSPIRACIES OF NAZI RACIST
HATRED THEY HAVE SEALED MY VAGINA

WITH MOLTEN LEAD AND LEFT ME TO DIE
ALONE THEY SEND MY CHILDREN BACK TO ME
DAILY IN MANILA LEGAL ENVELOPES

PIECE BY MYSTERIOUS PIECE DON'T BELIEVE
A WORD THEY TELL YOU PITY ME.
It is here I feel the first angina-constriction

Deep in the cardiac mind, and the *Nöos* says to the *Psyche,*
Watch where you go once you have entered here,
Which way and to whom you turn,

To which the *Kradie* answers, *That is not our concern.*
It is our fate to open every door. So I remember, now,
This is the real truth of it: I enter from every gate

At once, on every numbered street and avenue,
Jackson Heights, Mt. Eden, Bleeker, Lorimer, 59th—
And the enormity of my multitudinousness,

This apocalyptic rush hour, eclipses even the brilliance
Of the four quarters of the midnight city—
Regions with designations, attributes, and enumerations:

North the Quarter of the Vomiting Multitudes,
East the Quarter of Suppurations, *West*
The Quarter of the Pissing Millions, *South* the Quarter

Of Investment Banking—but before I can say them,
The great fluid weight of my entering
Washes me forward, and the silent electric doors

Of the silver cars open all together to take me in,
Every human soul of me at every intersection
In every borough of the city, bringing me in a thunderous

Convergence of superimposed switch-engines
Simultaneously *here,* to a level that demands me,
Grand Central Terminal, and the carriers disgorge me

In my statistical millions to circle
From platform to platform where the right trains
Never come. Every man and woman who was breathing

An instant ago must be with me now. Here is the tourist
From Michigan; she was staring at the Empire State
When a cloud of noxious oblivion touched her,

And she opened her eyes and was part of me.
Here is the lawyer from Queens; he knew the city
Inside out, but now he wanders this station

He passed through hundreds of times in his life
Wide-eyed and blank, dangling his forgotten briefcase
Like the ghost of a severed limb. Here is the man

Who bewildered, here is the child who devoured,
Here is the old Hindu woman who lived
Sweetly as a saint, and woke to this at ninety

From a heart-bursting sexual dream, the perfect
Circle of the caste mark between her eyes
Red as a cartoon bullet hole.

Here is the stockbroker, here is the stewardess,
Here is the crowd of girls with prep-school sweaters
And haloes of frosted hair who seem to be joined at the waist.

Here is the Chinese couple who juggled feathers
At the Lincoln Center Circus—they move
Their disciplined hands together, seeking a familiar balance.

Here is the Chilean ex-diplomat who went in fear
Of CIA assassins—to him these tiled walls
Have a beautiful coolness, he's never been so calm.

Here is the defrocked priest: forgetfulness
Has utterly altered him. Here is the ex-Reagan aide:
She seems completely unchanged.

And the Priestess of Greenwich Village,
And the slacker, and the dental assistant,
The majorette, the machinist, the freak, and the mother's son—

This is more than consent, or concord; it is a real
Unity of us all, in one and the same person,
Made by covenant of all of us with each of us, in such a manner

As if each of us should say to all of us, *I Authorize.*
I am a random human diorama, an outtake
From *The Night of the Living Dead.* This is my punishment

For forgetting to believe that blankness is the logical
Outcome of my passionate confusions. Now chaos darkens
The holy brightnesses of the unconscious world.

Overhead, signs light up to enumerate directions and destinations:
A Lake of Fire. A Bottomless Pit. A Horrible Tempest.
Everlasting Burnings. A Furnace of Fire. A Devouring Fire.

A Prison. A Place of Torments. A Place of Everlasting
Punishment. A Place where People Pray. A Place
Where they Scream for Mercy. A Place where they Wail.

A Place where they Curse God. In the vastnesses
Of Sotheby's, snuffboxes, folk arts, antiquities, toys,
Judaica, and other sacred artifacts take on

An unearthly luminosity—at the Village Gate,
The horns of fusion musicians synthesize and burn.
Now the imperious *Phrenes* begins to thrash

Far down in the shadows of the diaphragm,
The intercostal muscles of the rib cage, the smooth
Muscles surrounding the bronchial tubes

That regulate their bore, and so their resistance
To the passage of air—and beside it, or within it,
Its Siamese-twin doppelgänger image or other self,

The terrible *Thumos,* also snorts out of a primitive dream
Of breath-souls and the smooth interiors
Of ventricles and veins, black bile and yellow bile, mucous

And vitreous humors. They surface together
Like incestuous homoerotic lovers waking hours
Before sunrise, both blind and invisible,

Caught in a bedroom-darkness so profound
They might be sealed in the flesh-insulated cavity
Of one enormous torso. They begin their old dialogue,

The equivalent of the talk of husbands' and wives'
Did you hear a noise? Did you take out the garbage?
Did you pay the gas bill? Are the children murdered?—

But spoken in something other than words,
Whatever the language of nerves and corpuscles
Consists of, which cannot be rendered in the syntax

Of consciousness, but whose faintest echo
Translates roughly *{Phrenes} If the body vanishes,*
How can the spirit be broken? {Thumos} Don't ask.

Its scars leave residues. {Phrenes} But if it is the body
That breaks, how long does it take for the heartbeat
To calcify? {Thumos} Hush. Tell me the story

Of the place breath goes to survive
The suffocations we make for it. {Phrenes} It is a place
Where they can never repent, a place of weeping,

A place of sorrows, a place of outer darkness,
A place where they have no rest, a place of blackness
Or darkness forever, a place where their worm dieth not,

And fire is not quenched. {Thumos} And none of this is certain?
But nobody answers, for now the darkness modulates,
And I find I am in a space exterior to the body after all,

On a secret path along the rim of the starless city, perhaps,
Between the wall and the torments, or perhaps in a tunnel
Dug far below the other shafts, where I have been

Let down through a column that seems of brass,
Descended safely among the unhappy that I might witness
The vastation of souls. A multitude of pitiful

Men and woman are gargoyled by homelessness here,
Hung in various ways from the different parts of themselves
Corresponding to the sociology of their births.

And the *Thumos* says to the *Phrenes: Enumerate*
The ways the human body can be warped
By punishments, political or metapolitical, and how

Those punishments make allegories of suffering.
Do so succinctly, in an orderly way, clearly,
And giving examples. And the *Phrenes* offers up

This answer: *These are the measure for measure*
Hanging retributions against the disenfranchised:
Those who are Guilty of Passion

Or Cleanliness shall be hung by the pubic hair;
They shall be hung by the pierced thighs, Those
Who are Guilty of Standing Erect; by the eyes

Those who have Seen Things Clearly; by the nose
Those who Smell the Death of the Rat in the Wall;
Those Convicted of Worthiness shall be hoisted

By the reputation; Those Convicted of Intelligence
By the delicate inner skin of the wallet; by the tongue
Those who Know Poverty, Hunger, Color, or Charm;

By the ears Those who Learn the Direction
Of the Class Dialectic; by the genitals Those
Refused Credit; by the breasts Those Discovered

Suckling More of Their Own Kind; by the DNA,
Those who Combine Unfitness with Survival;
By the Phrenes, the Ones who are Poor and Disbelieve;

By the Thumos, the Ones who are Poor and Believe.
From the safety of my vantage point, I see
The truth of it all. The damned are ranged

Before me, row on blighted row. I approach the first
Prisoner or corpse or dead soul, a man dangled
By the tissues of the soft palate for the felony

Of his native tongue—he is effigied in the black rags
Of an ancient uniform of the Ohio National Guard,
His empty eye sockets ringed with kohl and stuffed

With planted Columbian Gold, the parchment
Of his forehead tattooed with the nine mystical numerals
Of the cabbala of Social Security

And the Kent State coat of arms. In horror
Of this blasphemous apparition, I fall back,
Nearly fainting, and stagger into a landscape

Where five hundred thousand blasted acres
Have been ripped apart by trenches and shells,
Villages cast down in ruins as if by earthquake,

Wounded trees, limbless and headless, looming
Above the desolation like scaffolds, the valley
A skeleton without flesh, save for the bodies

Of half a million dead ground up beneath the ceaseless
Bombardments. In insensible confusion, I stumble
On the misery of women moaning in parlors, in memory

Of the names of rivers their husbands died for—
The Nile, the Rhone, the Rhine, the Somme, the Marne,
The Aisne, the Yser, the Meuse, the Chickamauga,

The Yangtze, the Mekong, the Tigris and the Euphrates,
Where stealth bombers and F-111s vomit sulphur and acid
On the Mesopotamian plain until the image of my old father

Gilgamesh lurches out of the dust to lay hands on
The byzantine levers of a T-72 Soviet tank. One
Of these demons of unforgetting, a magnetized girl of twenty

Who lived sixty years beyond the day of her lover's desertion
By fuel-air bomb in the wreckage of Panama City,
Comes forward to comfort me with bandages and morphine,

Cool hands on the brow. The story of her girlhood
Materializes within me, an immaculate marriage
Of nightmare and menses. Now the voices of my stillborn

Sons and daughters rise from the blistered tarmac,
The strangled books of the vanished poets of America—
Lindsay, yes, and Sandburg, my binary idiot clones, but louder

I hear sweet Edwin Rolfe, whom no one now remembers:
John's deathbed is a curious affair, he is singing,
The posts are made of bone, the spring of nerves,

The mattress bleeding flesh. Infinite air,
Compressed from dizzy altitudes, now serves
His skullface as a pillow. In my drugged fever dream,

I am damned to the furious realm of Sol Funaroff, where
The earth smoked and baked; / stones in the field
Marked the dead land: coins taxing the earth,

And to Countee Cullen's crucifixion:
"Maybe God thinks such things are right."
"Maybe God never thinks at all. . . ."

It seems the body is scattered over the whole expanse
Of thought, arms and legs sliced away and dropped
Horribly into a pail, the circuitry of the nerves

Corroded, abdominal cavity looted for spare parts
And salvage, the *Kradie* and the *Ker*
At infinite removes from one another,

The *Psyche* bereft of the *Etor*—body and body politic
Forever dissevered, like precincts of the brain
In the wake of a bad lobotomy. I try to remember

Wholeness, the image of meadows in starlight,
Lovers in sentimental landscapes, glacier-capped
Purple-skewed mountains, the visionary wheathead

Held up by the Dionysian priest at Eleusis,
The imperious cliché of the sea, the splendid material love
Of Rukeyser—*I have gained mastery*

Over my heart / I have gained mastery
Over my two hands / I have gained mastery
Over the waters / I have gained mastery

Over the river—but it splinters in a billion diffractions,
Cells, dustmotes, atoms of asthmatic pollen,
Spume, sperm, fragments of quartzite, nitrogen,

Duct tape, cotter pins, subatomic wreckage,
Shreds of pointless false narratives left over
From childhood memories or from moon-illumined

Bedrooms where lovers defected from one another's countries.
This is the critical whirlwind. Nothing holds here.
I fracture again and again, giving in to every mythology.

The shattered ghosts come thick. Submicroscopic,
I seep through cracks in the nuclei,
An insidious multitudinous radioactive dust,

Undetectable by any instrument except as an oscillation
The cosmos emits at its own dismemberment
Into particles, into bodies carrying bowls of goats' blood,

Each going down into the hell of its own one-track mind.
Here is the ruptured anarchist soul
Of Arturo Giovanetti in prison, the one true confession

Of his poetry: *Wonderful is the supreme wisdom of the jail*
That makes all think the same thought. / Marvelous
Is the providence of the law that equalizes all, even

In mind and sentiment. / Fallen is the last barrier of privilege,
The aristocracy of the intellect. / I, who have never killed,
Think like the murderer; / I, who have never stolen, reason

Like the thief. What is this place where wisdom
Is an unnatural abomination, all knowledge is nature
Destroyed? How have I come to this perigee, where the heart

Is nothing but a spring, and the nerves but so many strings,
And the joints but so many wheels, giving motion
To the whole, as was intended by the artificer?

Here the larynx of Mike Gold, dipped in solder
And traced with magnificent circuitry, picks up the broadcast
His own crushed poems repeat into the emptiness

Like a satellite beacon: *I am resigning from the American legion*
It reminds me of a dog I used to have
That picked up toads in her mouth. . . .

Now, as the voices of these my emanations bark and bleed,
It is the intense strangeness of the world I want
To remember how to love—how it enters and exits

The body, air and æther and light—and to which I long
To return, thrown into being out of the center of being.
But what am I—an insulated ghost, appearance, apparition,

Epiphenomenon, holographic projection,
A comic book death's-head cast up on the shore
Of the living? Even this skin, which once trembled

At the thought of the touch of another human body,
Is unreal, only the projection of a vanished surface:
And the mind, when it falters and croaks—

I speak with authority now—loses its shape
As a bodily ego, follows the carcass
Cell by carrion cell, down through vegetable ooze

And crust and maggoty mantle and magma,
And arrives, in the innermost circle
Of the Republic of the Disappeared, at emptiness.

It was here, in the Land of the Metaphysically Free,
That, fallen, I dreamed my old America. By an act
Of most imperial will I assumed the Presidency of the Dead,

I shaped the ruptured shrapnel of my consciousness
Once more into a seedy mercenary army—
Phrenes and *Thumos* and *Nöos*

Commanding rank and file of the husks
Of riveters and lawyers (I gathered them
Tenderly as they settled), and residues of secretaries,

Dregs of ushers, gynecologists, thieves,
And the fine ash of Iraqi cabdrivers,
And the delicate grit of Marines,

Dust of Bush, Baker, Schwarzkopf, Cheney,
And beautiful Colin Powell: such a clay they made,
Such a multitude molded, such drum-taps and battle hymns.

At last I believed I understood them. At last
When I called their names they seemed
To shiver to hear me, as if they were almost alive.

But when I look now, there is only the finitude
Of nothing, only absence. I stand in the ultimate circle,
The innermost hell of all the hells, beyond

The outermost illusion: Purity, uncorrupted
Conscience, the body politic embracing
Self and nothing other, only the singular desire.

And as if at a mystical chime, or the alarm
Of a mineral clock, the subway signals ring again,
And I rush at the speed of darkness

From station to station, through the gnarly strata,
In among the tunnels of volcanic roots and sealed absolutes
Of salt domes, up along the nether edges

Of the limbo of Flushing, transformed at Queensboro Plaza
And again at Hoyt-Schermerhorn, to emerge at last
In mercuric February afternoon light

At the stairway marked *Brooklyn Bridge.*
Nothing has changed. Manhattan grinds on,
Gears of the living irreversibly meshed

With the ratchet of desire. There is still the apocalyptic
Discharge of cluster-bombs over the lower east side,
Brimstone of artillery out of the Village, sniper fire

From the Chrysler Building, the strafing
Of Bloomingdales. But everything on the earth I love
Is sealed from my touch as by a zone

Of Platonic plate glass. In my loneliness I rise
And hover over the plutonium-gray span
Of East River, licked by the harrowing fallout

Of my own intangibility. From here I can see,
Like a skyline, the obvious contour of all
My error. O I freely confess it now: America,

I was wrong. I am only slightly larger than life.
I contain mere conspiracies. What do I know?
There is no identity at the basis of things, no one

Name beneath all names. There is no more than this
To remember: *It is not godlike to die. It is not even human.*
Refuse the honor, no matter who tells you its conquest is sublime.

I may have mumbled that old lie myself once.
I have confessed to many things. Maybe that is why I am
The only one dead here. Maybe that is why I have to suffer

Everything I can. Maybe that is why—
Over the unconscious roofs of your living
Beauty shops, sweatshops, pawnshops, printshops, meat shops,

Warehouses, bathhouses, crackhouses, penthouses, card houses—
Once and for all unhearable, and for all I know unthinkable, I go on
Sounding my doomed eternal bodiless goddamned

I, I, I, I, I.

Notes

"Zeitgeist Lightning": Justin Kaplan's *Walt Whitman: A Life* (Simon and Shuster, 1980) gives the following account of the fate of Walt Whitman's brain: After Whitman's death, Whitman's brother George "refused to allow the autopsy; the doctors waited until he left the house that afternoon and then went ahead with their work. . . . The doctors removed his brain and sent it to be measured and weighed at the American Anthropometric Society, where it was destroyed when a laboratory worker accidentally dropped it on the floor."

"The Heavenly Eunuchs of Rochester": The quote in part iv is from Sartre's *The Age of Reason,* translated by Eric Sutton (Vintage, 1973).

"Ohio Abstract: Hart Crane": I'm indebted for biographical information (for instance, the fact that Hart Crane's father was a successful manufacturer of fancy chocolates, who invented Lifesavers candy, but sold the idea cheaply to another company because that sort of product was beneath his dignity) to John Unterecker's *Voyager: A Life of Hart Crane* (Liveright, 1969).

"My Funny Valentine in Spanish": The quote from Neruda that closes the poem is from Donald D. Walsh's translation of "I Explain a Few Things" in *Residencies on Earth* (New Directions, 1973). I also owe thanks to Philip Levine for his help in settling on the best non-translation into Spanish of the phrase "my funny valentine."

"The Antichrist in Arkansas": Material is borrowed from Elaine Pagels, *The Gnostic Gospels* (Vintage, 1979).

"The Heavenly Doctor": Various phrases are lifted, and twisted, from *Dr. Colmer's Journals: A Daily Diary of a Springfield* [Louisiana] *Physician, originally from England, Who Recorded Items of Interest from Experimenting Growing Vegetables to Being Part of History Shortly After the Creation of Livingston Parish,* compiled and edited by Warren B. Wall (Ellzey Publications, 1986).

"Greek": The quote from Homer's *Iliad* is Richmond Lattimore's translation. Quotes from Euclid are John Playfair's translation (W. E. Dean, 1845), from a leatherbound high-school textbook I inherited from the library of my great-grandfather T. W. Jackson (1860–1957), who remembered the Civil War and told me stories about it when I was a boy.

"Worldly Beauty": Descriptions of tattoos and tattooing are loosely based on Smithsonian Institute reports of religious practices of the Maori.

"Walt Whitman in Hell": Besides the obvious debts this poem owes to Whitman and Dante, a good many other sources were also dissolved into the body of the text in the four years its composition required, including the following: *Heaven and Its Wonders and Hell: From Things Heard and Seen,* by Emmanuel Swedenborg; *Poet in New York,* by Federico Garcia Lorca, translated by Ben Belitt (Grove, 1955); *Leviathan,* by Thomas Hobbes; *Tours of Hell: An Apocalyptic Form in Jewish and Christian Literature,* by Martha Himmelfarb (Fortress Press, 1985); a pamphlet, "Hell: What Is It?" (Tract Evangelistic Crusade, Box 998 Apache Junction, Arizona 85220), containing an exhaustive list of biblical descriptions, which was handed to me by a street preacher at an entrance of the New York subway; *The Culture of Redemption,* by Leo Bersani (Harvard, 1990); Michel Foucault's *The History of Sexuality,* translated by Robert Hurley (Vintage, 1980); and (for some of the quotes from "forgotten" poets) *Repression and Recovery: Modern American Poetry and the Politics of Cultural Memory, 1910–1945,* by Cary Nelson (University of Wisconsin, 1989).